JOHN STOTT BIBLE STUDIES

18 Studies with Commentary for Individuals or Groups

Acts

Seeing the Spirit at Work

John
STOTT

with Phyllis J. Le Peau

Inter-Varsity Press
Nottingham, England

IVP Connect
An imprint of InterVarsity Press
Downers Grove, Illinois

InterVarsity Press, USA
P.O. Box 1400, Downers Grove, IL 60515-1426, USA
World Wide Web: www.ivpress.com
Email: email@ivpress.com

Inter-Varsity Press, England
Norton Street, Nottingham NG7 3HR, England
Website: www.ivpbooks.com
Email: ivp@ivpbooks.com

InterVarsity Press®, USA, is the book-publishing division of InterVarsity Christian Fellowship/USA®,
a student movement active on campus at hundreds of universities, colleges and schools of nursing in
the United States of America, and a member movement of the International Fellowship of Evangelical
Students. For information about local and regional activities, write Public Relations Dept., InterVarsity
Christian Fellowship/USA, 6400 Schroeder Rd., P.O. Box 7895, Madison, WI 53707-7895, or visit the IVCF
website at <www.intervarsity.org>.

Inter-Varsity Press, England, is closely linked with the Universities and Colleges Christian Fellowship, a
student movement connecting Christian Unions in universities and colleges throughout Great Britain, and
a member movement of the International Fellowship of Evangelical Students. Website: www.uccf.org.uk.

This study guide is based on and includes excerpts adapted from The Message of Acts ©1990 by John R.
W. Stott, originally published under the title The Spirit, the Church and the World.

Design: Cindy Kiple
Images: Digital Zoo/Getty Images

USA ISBN 978-0-8308-2161-7
UK ISBN 978-1-84474-316-2

Printed in the United States of America ∞

P   23   22   21   20   19   18   17   16   15   14   13   12   11   10   9   8   7   6   5   4   3

Y   27   26   25   24   23   22   21   20   19   18   17   16   15   14   13   12   11   10   09

Introducing Acts

The introduction to Acts makes it clear that Acts is the second book written by Luke. The two form an obvious pair. Luke does not regard volume one as the story of Jesus Christ from his birth through his sufferings and death to his triumphant resurrection and ascension, and volume two as the story of the church of Jesus Christ. For the contrasting parallel he draws is not between Christ and his church, but between two stages of the ministry of the same Christ. In his former book he has written about all that Jesus began to do and to teach until the day he was taken up to heaven. In this his second book he will write about what Jesus continued to do and to teach after his ascension, especially through the apostles. Thus Jesus' ministry on earth was followed by his ministry from heaven, exercised through his Holy Spirit by his apostles.

Getting to Know Luke
Luke claims to write accurate history based on the reports of eyewitnesses; Roman historians have long taken it for granted. Luke was well qualified to write history as an educated doctor and a traveling companion of Paul's. Even in those days doctors underwent quite a rigorous training, and Luke's stylish Greek is that of a cultured person.

Luke's volumes are addressed to Theophilus. He may have been a Roman offical who had heard anti-Christian slanders. Luke repeatedly forms a political apologetic to show Christianity was harmless (because some Roman officials had embraced it themselves), innocent (because Roman judges could find no basis for prosecution) and lawful (because it was the true fulfillment of Judaism).

Luke was also a peacemaker in the church. He wanted to demonstrate that the early church was united, that the peril of division between Jewish and Samaritan Christians, and between Jewish and Gentile Christians, was providentially avoided, and that the apostles Peter, James and Paul were in fundamental agreement about the gospel.

A Message for Us

In Acts Luke proclaims the gospel of salvation from God in Christ for all people. This is why he includes so many sermons and addresses, especially by Peter and Paul. He not only shows them preaching to their original hearers, but also enables them to preach to us who, centuries later, listen to them. For as Peter said on the day of Pentecost, the promise of salvation is for us too, and for every generation, indeed "for all whom the Lord our God will call" (Acts 2:39).

Suggestions for Individual Study

1. As you begin each study, pray that God will speak to you through his Word.

2. Read the introduction to the study and respond to the question that follows it. This is designed to help you get into the theme of the study.

3. The studies are written in an inductive format designed to help you discover for yourself what Scripture is saying. Each study deals with a particular passage so that you can really delve into the author's meaning in that context. Read and reread the passage to be studied. The questions are written using the language of the New International Version, so you may wish to use that version of the Bible. The New Revised Standard Version is also recommended.

4. Each study includes three types of questions. *Observation* questions ask about the basic facts: who, what, when, where and how. *Interpretation* questions delve into the meaning of the passage. *Application* questions (also found in the "Apply" section) help you discover the implications of the text for growing in Christ. These three keys unlock the treasures of Scripture.

Write your answers to the study questions in the spaces provided or in a personal journal. Writing can bring clarity and deeper understanding of yourself and of God's Word.

5. In the studies you will find some commentary notes designed to give help with complex verses by giving further biblical and cultural background and contextual information. The notes in the studies are not designed to answer the questions for you. They are to help you along as you learn to study the Bible for yourself. After you have worked through the questions and notes in the guide, you may want to read the accompanying commentary by John Stott in the Bible Speaks Today series. This will give you more information about the text.

6. Move to the "Apply" section. These questions will help you connect the key biblical themes to your own life. Putting the application into practice is one of the keys to growing in Christ.

7. Use the guidelines in the "Pray" section to focus on God, thanking him for what you have learned and praying about the applications that have come to mind.

Suggestions for Members of a Group Study

1. Come to the study prepared. Follow the suggestions for individual study mentioned above. You will find that careful preparation will greatly enrich your time spent in group discussion.

2. Be willing to participate in the discussion. The leader of your group will not be lecturing. Instead, she or he will be encouraging the members of the group to discuss what they have learned. The leader will be asking the questions that are found in this guide.

3. Stick to the topic being discussed. Your answers should be based on the verses which are the focus of the discussion and not on outside authorities such as commentaries or speakers. These studies focus on a particular passage of Scripture. Only rarely should you refer to other portions of the Bible. This allows for everyone to participate on equal ground and for in-depth study.

4. Be sensitive to the other members of the group. Listen attentively when they describe what they have learned. You may be surprised by their insights! Each question assumes a variety of answers. Many questions do not have "right" answers, particularly questions that aim at meaning or application. Instead the questions push us to explore the passage more thoroughly.

When possible, link what you say to the comments of others. Also, be affirming whenever you can. This will encourage some of the more hesitant members of the group to participate.

5. Be careful not to dominate the discussion. We are sometimes so eager to express our thoughts that we leave too little opportunity for others to respond. By all means participate! But allow others to also.

6. Expect God to teach you through the passage being discussed and through the other members of the group. Pray that you will have an enjoyable and profitable time together, but also that as a result of the study you will find ways that you can take action individually and/or as a group.

7. It will be helpful for groups to follow a few basic guidelines. These guidelines, which you may wish to adapt to your situation, should be read at the beginning of the first session.

☐ Anything said in the group is considered confidential and will not be discussed outside the group unless specific permission is given to do so.

☐ We will provide time for each person present to talk if he or she feels comfortable doing so.

☐ We will talk about ourselves and our own situations, avoiding conversation about other people.

☐ We will listen attentively to each other.

☐ We will be very cautious about giving advice.

8. If you are the group leader, you will find additional suggestions at the back of the guide.

1
WAITING
FOR THE SPIRIT

Acts 1

*T*imes. Dates. We want to know when Jesus will return. So did the apostles. In Acts 1 they were asking, "Lord, are you at this time going to restore the kingdom to Israel?" (v. 6).

Jesus told the disciples that they were not to know times or dates, but what they should know was that they would receive power so that, between the Spirit's coming at Pentecost and the Son's coming again, they could be his witnesses in ever-widening circles. In fact, the whole interim period between Pentecost and Jesus' return is to be filled with the worldwide mission of the church in the power of the Spirit. Christ's followers were both to announce what he had achieved at his first coming and to summon people to be his witnesses "to the ends of the earth" (1:8).

Christ's vision and commission would give clear direction to the disciple's prayers during their ten days of waiting for Pentecost. But before the Spirit could come, the Son must go. The themes of Acts 1 will encourage and instruct all who wait for Jesus.

Open

■ What helps you to feel equipped to carry out Jesus' ministry on earth?

Study

■ *Read Acts 1:1-5.* Luke's first two verses are extremely significant. It is no exaggeration to say that they set Christianity apart from other religions that regard their founder as having completed his ministry during his lifetime. Luke says Jesus only began his. This is the kind of Jesus Christ we believe in: both the historical Jesus who lived and the contemporary Jesus who lives.

1. In what ways did Jesus prepare and equip his apostles to continue his ministry and life on earth?

2. What was the significance of the fact that Jesus showed himself to the apostles and gave many convincing proofs that he was alive?

3. How would the apostles' ministry be affected by the fact that Jesus chose, commissioned and instructed them?

Summary: In a sense all the disciples of Jesus can claim that he has chosen us, revealed himself to us, commissioned us as his witnesses, and both promised and given us his Spirit. Nevertheless, it is not to these general privileges that Luke is referring here, but to the special qualifications of an apostle—a personal appointment as an apostle by Jesus, an eyewitness experience of the historical Jesus, an authorizing and commissioning by Jesus to speak in his name, and the empowering Spirit of Jesus to inspire their teaching. It was primarily these uniquely qualified men through whom Jesus continued "to do and to teach," and to whom Luke intends to introduce us in the Acts.

---

4. *Read Acts 1:6-11.* What evidence is there that the disciples did not understand the kingdom that Jesus set up?

---

5. The primary way that Jesus equipped the apostles was the promise of the Holy Spirit. What was going to be the result of the Holy Spirit coming on them?

The major event of the early chapters of the Acts took place on the day of Pentecost, when the now-exalted Lord Jesus performed the last work of his saving career (until his coming again) and "poured" out the Holy Spirit on his waiting people. His life, death, resurrection and ascension all culminated in the great gift, which the prophets had foretold and which would be recognized as the chief evidence that God's kingdom had been inaugurated. For this conclusion of Christ's work on earth was also a fresh beginning. Just as the Spirit came upon Jesus to equip him for his public ministry, so now the Spirit was to come upon his people to equip them for theirs.

6. What difference would the ascension of Jesus and the promise of his return make in the ministry of the apostles?

---

7. *Read Acts 1:12-26.* Why do you think prayer seemed to be the major activity that they engaged in after they returned?

Luke tells us that their prayers had two characteristics, which, Calvin comments, are "two essentials for true prayer, namely that they persevered, and were of one mind" (*Acts of the Apostles,* vol. I [1552, Oliver and Boyd, 1965], p. 38). There can be little doubt that the grounds of this unity and perseverance in prayer were the command and promise of Jesus. He had promised to send them the Spirit soon (1:4-5, 8). He had commanded them to wait for him to come and then to begin their witness. We learn, therefore, that God's promises do not remove the need for prayer. On the contrary, it is only his promises which give us the warrant to pray and the confidence that he will hear and answer.

---

8. What was Peter's conclusion about Judas (vv. 15-20)?

9. What were the qualifications of the person who would replace Judas (vv. 21-26)?

10. Why were these qualifications important?

Summary: The stage is now set for the day of Pentecost. The apostles have received Christ's commission and seen his ascension. The apostolic team is complete again, ready to be his chosen witnesses. Only one thing is missing: the Spirit has not yet come. So we leave Luke's first chapter of Acts with the 120 waiting in Jerusalem, persevering in prayer with one heart and mind, poised ready to fulfill Christ's command just as soon as he has fulfilled his promise.

Apply ———————————————————————————
■ The records of these acts of the Holy Ghost have never reached completeness. This is the one book which has no proper close, because it waits for new chapters to be added so fast and so far as the people of God shall reinstate the blessed Spirit in his holy seat of control. How are you involved in being and praying for the witness of Jesus throughout the world, beginning with your own "Jerusalem"?

How have you seen the power of the Holy Spirit in the ministry of others?

in your own life?

How would you like to experience more of his power?

Pray

■ Praise God for the provision that he has made for you to be his witness. Ask him to empower you for that task.

2
RECEIVING
THE SPIRIT

Acts 2

*W*ithout the Holy Spirit, Christian discipleship would be inconceivable, even impossible. There can be no life without the life-giver, no understanding without the Spirit of Truth, no fellowship without the unity of the Spirit, no Christlikeness of character apart from his fruit, and no effective witness without his power. As a body without breath is a corpse, so the church without the Spirit is dead. Luke is well aware of this and emphasizes the power of the Spirit throughout Acts, especially in Acts 2, which is all about the day of Pentecost, when the Spirit comes.

Open

■ What difference do you think it would make if the Holy Spirit were withdrawn from your life and your Christian community?

Study

■ *Read Acts 2:1-13.* Pentecost brought to the apostles what they needed for their special role. Christ had appointed them to be his primary and authoritative witnesses and had promised them the reminding and teaching ministry of the Holy Spirit.

Pentecost was the inauguration of the new era of the Spirit. Although his coming was a unique and unrepeatable historical event, all the people of God can now always and everywhere benefit from his ministry.

---

1. Describe in detail, as if you were a reporter covering an important story, what happened on the day of Pentecost.

---

2. What were the different reactions to these events?

---

3. When Luke spoke of the international nature of the crowd which collected, he was speaking from his own horizon—the Greco-Roman world situated around the Mediterranean basin, every nation in which there were Jews. This was the international, multilingual crowd which gathered around the 120 believers. Why do you think Luke emphasizes this fact?

Discussion about the nature of speaking in tongues must not distract our attention from Luke's understanding of its significance on the day of Pentecost. It symbolized a new unity in the Spirit transcending racial, national and linguistic barriers. Ever since the early church fathers, commentators have seen the blessing of Pentecost as a deliberate and dramatic reversal of the curse of Babel.

4. *Read Acts 2:14-41.* What do you observe about Peter as he addresses the crowd?

5. How does Peter explain these amazing events that have taken place at Pentecost?

The best way to understand Pentecost is not through the Old Testament prediction, but through the New Testament fulfillment, not through Joel but through Jesus. As Peter summons the men of Israel to listen to him, his first words are of Jesus of Nazareth, and he goes on to tell the story of Jesus in six stages: his life and ministry, his death, his resurrection, his exaltation, his salvation and his new community.

Peter's conclusion is that all Israel should be assured that this Jesus, whom they had repudiated and crucified, God had made both Lord and Christ. Not of course that Jesus became Lord and Christ only at the time of his ascension, for he was (and claimed to be) both throughout his public ministry. It is rather that now God exalted him to be in reality and power what he already was by right.

7. On what basis does Peter announce that God has made this Jesus both Lord and Christ (vv. 29-36)?

8. How did the people respond to Peter's clear proclamation of the truth about Jesus and the truth about themselves (vv. 37-41)?

9. Based on the information given in this passage, how would you summarize the message of Jesus?

10. *Read Acts 2:42-47.* What are the spiritual and practical results of the outpouring of the Spirit?

Summary: Our struggle is how to be faithful to this apostolic gospel while at the same time presenting it in a way which resonates with men and women today. What is immediately clear is that, like the apostles, we must focus on Jesus Christ. Peter's beginning "Listen to this: Jesus . . ." must be our beginning too. But how? I have myself found it an aid to faithfulness to express the apostles' message in the following framework: the gospel events, namely the death and resurrection of Jesus, the gospel witnesses, the Scriptures and the apostles, the gospel promises, the forgiveness of sin and the Spirit, and the gospel conditions, repentance with faith and baptism.

It is not enough to "proclaim Jesus." For there are many different Jesuses being presented today. According to the New Testament gospel, however, he is historical (he really lived, died, rose and ascended in the arena of history), theological (his life, death, resurrection and ascension all have saving significance) and contemporary (he lives and reigns to bestow salvation on those who respond to him). Thus the apostles told the same story of Jesus at three levels—as historical event (witnessed by their own eyes), as having theological significance (interpreted by the Scriptures), and as contemporary message (confronting men and women with the necessity of decision). We have the same responsibility today to tell the story of Jesus as fact, doctrine and gospel.

Apply ————————————————————————

■ How do you respond to the work and power of the Holy Spirit as you see it in this chapter?

When have you seen and experienced the work of the Spirit in your life and Christian community?

What do you need to do in order to more effectively proclaim the truth about Jesus to those who may not know him as the Lord and Christ?

Pray

■ Praise God for the work and power of his Holy Spirit. Ask him to teach you to understand and rely on his ministry.

3
THE OUTBREAK
OF PERSECUTION

Acts 3:1—4:31

*J*esus has returned to heaven before the very eyes of the astounded disciples. Matthias has been chosen to replace Judas. The Holy Spirit has descended upon the earth with great power and in ways that cannot be explained away by the religious leaders. Thousands are coming to Jesus. The believers of Jesus are together in love, fellowship and meeting each other's needs. Instead of the world rejoicing and embracing with open arms all the good things God is doing, resistance begins to build.

This resistance to the gospel of Jesus Christ continues today. The church needs to observe and learn from the early church how to remain faithful and active in the proclamation of truth, even though the cost is great—through the power of the Holy Spirit. Although the coming of the Spirit was a unique and unrepeatable historical event, all the people of God can now always and everywhere benefit from his ministry.

Open ─────────────────────────────

■ When have you been persecuted for living or proclaiming truth about Jesus?

Study

■ *Read Acts 3:1-10.* What triggered the opposition of the Jewish authorities was the healing of the cripple, together with Peter's sermon which followed it. Luke began his second volume by telling his readers that he was going to record what Jesus continued "to do and to teach" through his apostles (1:1-2). He has also told us that "many wonders and miraculous signs were done by the apostles" (2:43). Now he supplies a particular, dramatic example.

1. Describe, as if you were there looking on, what happened between Peter and John and the man who was crippled from birth.

2. How did the crippled man respond?

How did all the people respond?

Peter seized the opportunity to preach. Just as the Pentecost event had been the text for his first sermon, so the cripple's healing became the text for his second. Both were mighty acts of the exalted Christ. Both were signs which proclaimed him Lord and Savior. Both aroused the crowd's amazement.

3. *Read Acts 3:11-26.* The most remarkable feature of Peter's second sermon, as of his first, is its Christ-centeredness. He directed the crowd's attention away from both the healed cripple and the apostles to the Christ. What vital points did Peter make in his sermon to the crowd?

---

4. Look at each of the titles Peter gives to Jesus. How do each of these speak to the uniqueness of Jesus?

---

5. Peter ends his sermon by challenging his hearers with the necessity of repentance. What blessings would follow if they repented (vv. 19-26)?

---

6. *Read Acts 4:1-22.* What do we learn about the attitude of the religious leaders toward Peter and John?

---

7. Peter has given a comprehensive testimony to Jesus as rejected by humanity but vindicated by God, as the fulfillment of all Old Testament prophecy, as demanding repentance and promising blessing, and as the author and giver of life, physically to the healed cripple and spiritually to those who believe. This aroused the indignation and antagonism of the authorities. Why do you think this proclamation of Jesus was disturbing to the religious leaders?

---

8. How would you explain the connection between the healed cripple and salvation (vv. 9-12)?

---

9. What evidence do you see of the power of the Holy Spirit throughout this section?

---

10. *Read Acts 4:23-31.* Describe the prayer in these verses.

How is it different than you would expect it to be after all that Peter and John had been through?

11. List the three requests in verses 29-30. What is the significance of these requests?

---

12. Why were they able to respond to persecution in this way?

Summary: We observe that before the people came to any petition, they filled their minds with thoughts of the divine sovereignty. First, he is the God of creation, who made the heaven and the earth and the sea, and everything in them (v. 24). Second, he is the God of revelation, who spoke by the Holy Spirit through the mouth of David, and in Psalm 2 (already in the first century B.C. recognized as Messianic) had foretold the world's opposition to his Christ, with nations raging, peoples plotting, kings standing and rulers assembling against the Lord's Anointed (vv. 25-26). Third, he is the God of history, who had caused even his enemies (Herod and Pilate, Gentiles and Jews, united in a conspiracy against Jesus, v. 27) to do what his power and will had decided beforehand should happen (v. 28). This, then, was the early church's understanding of God, the God of creation, revelation and history, whose characteristic actions are summarized by the three verbs *made* (v. 24), *spoke* (v. 25), and *decided* (v. 28).

Apply ——————————————————————————
■ When have you seen resistance, subtle or overt, to the gospel of Christ?

What truth from this passage equips you to face this resistance?

Who is suffering persecution for the gospel that you could be praying for?

Pray————————————————————————

■ Praise the Lord Jesus for who he is and specifically for what is revealed about him in this passage. Ask the Holy Spirit to prepare you for and minister through you in persecution.

4
SATANIC COUNTERATTACK

Acts 4:32 – 6:7

*T*hroughout the world today, thousands are suffering and dying for Jesus. During the twentieth century, more Christians have been killed, either directly for their faith or in situations where being a Christian has played a role in violent confrontations, than in all the other centuries combined. Where there is life and growth, Satan will attack.

As soon as the Spirit came upon the church (Acts 3), Satan launched a ferocious counterattack. While it is true that his first and crudest tactic is physical violence, crushing the church by persecution, his second is even more cunning: moral corruption and compromise. This form of attack makes sense because Christ is exalted by the integrity of his church. The early church was not exempt. The first example in Scripture of the attempt to insinuate evil into the interior life of the church is the story of Ananias and Sapphira.

Open ————————————————————————

■ How do you respond to the idea that Satan is attacking the church today?

1. *Read Acts 4:32—5:11.* In Acts 4:31 we see that the prayer of the believers was answered and they were freshly filled with the Holy Spirit and spoke the word of God boldly. What evidence do you see of this filling of the Spirit in verses 32-36?

Calvin wrote in *The Acts of the Apostles* (vol. 1, p. 130):

We must have hearts that are harder than iron if we are not moved by the reading of this narrative. In those days the believers gave abundantly of what was their own; we in our day are content not just jealously to retain what we possess, but callously to rob others. . . . They sold their own possessions in those days; in our day it is the lust to purchase that reigns supreme. At that time love made each man's own possessions common property for those in need; in our day such is the inhumanity of many, that they begrudge to the poor a common dwelling upon earth, the common use of water, air and sky.

2. What could your church or fellowship group learn from this example?

3. Now look closely at the story of Ananias and Sapphira. Why do you think their offenses were so grave?

4. Luke clearly intends us to understand that the death of Ananias and Sapphira was a work of divine judgment. How do you respond to the severity of God's judgment?

There are at least three valuable lessons for us to learn. First, the gravity of their sin. Peter stressed this by repeating that their lie was not directed primarily against him, but against the Holy Spirit, that is, against God. And God hates hypocrisy.

Second, the importance, even sacredness, of the human conscience. This seems to be what John meant by "walking in the light." It is to live a transparent life before God. In East African it is said that we are "to live in a house without ceiling or walls," that is, to permit nothing to come between us and either God or other people.

Third, the incident teaches the necessity of church discipline. The church has tended to oscillate in this area between extreme severity and extreme laxity. It is a good general rule that private sins should be dealt with privately and public sins and only public sins, publicly. Churches are also wise if they follow the successive stages taught by Jesus. Usually the offender will be brought to repentance before the final stage of excommunication.

---

5. Which of these lessons strikes you as something we need to learn today?

6. *Read Acts 5:12-41.* What were the various responses to the ministry of the apostles?

7. What reasons do you find for the actions that the high priests took?

8. What do you learn from this passage about obeying human authority and obeying divine authority?

9. Describe the effect of persecution on the apostles (vv. 41-42).

The devil's next attack was the cleverest of the three. Having failed to overcome the church by either persecution or corruption, he now tried distraction. If he could preoccupy the apostles with social administration, which though essential was not their calling, they would neglect their God-given responsibilities to pray and to preach, and so leave the church without any defense against false doctrine.

10. *Read Acts 6:1-7.* What principles do you see about the way the church should function in relationship to problem-solving?

in relationship to call to ministry?

11. The apostles delegated the social work in order to concentrate on their pastoral priority. What were the results of this action?

Summary: The devil exists and is utterly unscrupulous. Something else about him is that he is peculiarly lacking in imagination. Over the years he has changed neither his strategy, nor his tactics, nor his weapons; he is still in the same old rut. So a study of his campaign against the early church should alert us to his probable strategy today. If we are taken by surprise, we shall have no excuse.

Luke is concerned, however, not only to expose the devil's malice, but also to show how he was overcome. First, the hypocrisy of Ananias and Sapphira was not allowed to spread, for God's judgment fell on them, and the church grew by leaps and bounds (5:12-16). Second, when the Sanhedrin again resorted to violence, they were restrained from killing the apostles by the cautious counsel of Gamaliel (5:17-42). Third, when the widows' dispute threatened to occupy all the time and energies of the apostles, the social work was delegated to others, the apostles resumed their priority tasks, and the church again began to multiply (6:1-7).

Apply
■ What can you learn from observing the effects of persecution on the church?

How might you become a more effective member of your church or fellowship as a result of what you have studied in this passage?

Pray
■ Praise God for the faithfulness of the apostles in preaching the word and prayer. Thank God for the church that God has placed you in. Ask God to help you grow in becoming a member of his church, full of integrity and commitment.

5
STEPHEN THE MARTYR

Acts 6:8—7:60

*S*tephen was the first. Many have followed in his steps to martyrdom—those who live and speak truth that is intolerable on this planet of evil. Stephen was described as full of the Spirit and wisdom, full of grace and power. When enemies of the message of Jesus could not stand up against this Spirit and wisdom, they stoned him to death. Stephen was a gift to the church but could not be tolerated by her enemies.

Stephen's greatest gift to the church was not the mere fact that he was her first martyr, but also his vital role in promoting the mission and the life of the church.

Open
■ How do you respond to the possibility of dying because you are a follower of Jesus?

Study
1. *Read Acts 6:8-15.* What do you learn about Stephen?

2. What were the accusations made against Stephen (6:13-14)?

The accusations against Stephen were extremely serious. Nothing was more sacred to the Jews, and nothing more precious, than their temple and their law. The temple was their "holy place," the sanctuary of God's presence, and the law was "holy scripture," the revelation of God's mind and will. Therefore, since the temple was God's house and the law was God's word, to speak against either was to speak against God or, in other words, to blaspheme.

---

3. *Read Acts 7:1-53.* When asked if the charges were true, Stephen responded with a sermon. List the people mentioned and the part they play in the history he is retelling (briefly).

Person   **Key Facts**

Stephen needed to defend himself against them in such a way as to develop a defense for his radical gospel. What he did was not just to rehearse the key features of the Old Testament story, with which the Sanhedrin were as familiar as he, but to do so in such a way as to draw lessons from it which they had never learned or even noticed. His concern was to demonstrate that his position, far from being "blasphemous" because disrespectful to God's Word, actually honored it. For Old Testament Scripture itself confirmed his teaching about the temple and the law, especially by predicting the Messiah, whereas by rejecting him it was they who disregarded the law, not he. Stephen's mind had evidently soaked up the Old Testament, for his speech is like a patchwork of allusions to it.

---

4. What was God's promise to Abraham, and how did he fulfill this promise (7:5, 17, 30, 36)?

---

5. How does Stephen communicate his respect for Moses (7:20, 22, 30-38)?

---

6. How did the people respond to Moses in the wilderness (7:39-43)?

---

7. What is the significance of the words "Take off your sandals; the place where you are standing is holy ground" (7:33), and "The Most High does not live in houses made by men" (7:48)?

Several psalms bear witness to Israel's love for the temple. This was right. But many drew a false conclusion. They conceived of God as so completely identified with the temple that its existence guaranteed his protection of them, while its destruction would mean that he had abandoned them. Long before them, however, as Stephen pointed out, the great figures of the Old Testament never imagined that God was imprisoned in a building. The God of Israel is a pilgrim God, who is not restricted to any one place. If he has any home on earth, it is with his people that he lives. He has pledged himself by a solemn covenant to be their God. Therefore, according to his covenant promise, wherever they are, there he is also.

---

8. How did Stephen's sermon speak to the accusations against him?

---

9. How are Stephen's accusers guilty of that which they accused him (7:51-53)?

---

10. *Read Acts 7:54-60.* What do you discover about Stephen's character in this section?

---

11. How did Stephen promote the mission and life of the church?

Summary: What interests many people most about Stephen is that he was the first Christian martyr. Luke's main concern lies elsewhere, however. He emphasizes the vital role Stephen played in the development of the worldwide Christian mission through both his teaching and his death. Stephen's martyrdom supplemented the influence of his teaching. Not only did it deeply impress Saul of Tarsus and contribute to his conversion, which led to his becoming the apostle to the Gentiles, but it was also the start of "a great persecution" which led to the scattering of the disciples "throughout Judea and Samaria" (8:1).

The church was shocked, even stunned by the martyrdom of Stephen and by the violent opposition which followed. But, with the benefit of hindsight, we can see how God's providence used Stephen's testimony in word and deed, through life and death, to promote the church's mission.

Apply
■ When have you experienced being "on holy ground"?

In what ways are you, like the Israelites in the wilderness, tempted to turn your heart back toward Egypt?

There are several parallels between the death of Jesus and the death of Stephen. In both cases false witnesses were produced and the charge was one of blasphemy. In both cases the execution was accompanied by two prayers, as each prayed for the forgiveness of his executioners and for the reception of his spirit as he died. Thus did the disciple—whether consciously or unconsciously—reflect his Master. The only difference was that

Jesus addressed his prayers to the Father, while Stephen addressed them to Jesus, calling him "Lord" and putting him on a level with God.

How would you like the way in which you follow Jesus to be influenced by Stephen's example?

Pray ——————————————————————————————

■ Ask the Holy Spirit to keep you steadfast, having always in mind his will and mission for the world and the church.

6
PHILIP
THE EVANGELIST

Acts 8:1-40

*I*n his continued warfare against the church the devil finally overreached himself. His attack had the opposite effect to what he intended. Instead of smothering the gospel, persecution succeeded only in spreading it.

Beginning the day of Stephen's death, persecution broke out with the ferocity of a sudden storm. Saul, who approved of Stephen's stoning, now began to destroy the church. This great persecution led to great dispersion: all except the apostles were scattered. The scattering of the Christians was followed by the scattering of the good seed of the gospel. For those who scattered preached the word wherever they went.

So we see in the midst of persecution wonderful things have happened. The Holy Spirit has revealed himself in mighty and miraculous ways. He has caused men and women to come to Jesus and the church to grow. We have seen him severely discipline a couple who lied to God and pretended to be something that they were not. We have witnessed men full of the Spirit both preaching Christ and dying for him. Now we are going to look at his work in Philip, who was filled with the Spirit and called by the Spirit away from "where the action was" to share the good news about Jesus with one individual—an Ethiopian.

Open

■ Do you see yourself as an evangelist? Explain.

Study ————————————————————————

1. *Read Acts 8:1-25.* In this chapter the command to be witnesses is Judea and Samaria (see Acts 1:8) is fulfilled. What are the causes and extent of the spread of the gospel?

The hostility between Jews and Samaritans had lasted a thousand years. It began with the monarchy in the tenth century B.C. when ten tribes defected, making Samaria their capital, and only two tribes remained loyal to Jerusalem. It became steadily worse when Samaria was captured by Assyria in 722 B.C. Thousands of its inhabitants were deported, and the country was repopulated by foreigners. In the sixth century B.C., when the Jews returned to their land, they refused the help of the Samaritans in the rebuilding of the temple. Not till the fourth century B.C., however, did the Samaritan schism harden, with the building of their rival temple on Mount Gerizim and their rejection of all Old Testament Scripture except the Pentateuch. The Samaritans were despised by the Jews.

---

2. How is it significant that Philip, a Jew, went to Samaria (v. 5)?

---

3. How was Simon the Sorcerer's life affected by the gospel (vv. 9-13)?

4. What did Peter teach Simon about following Jesus (vv. 18-24)?

5. Why do you think it was important for the church in Jerusalem to send Peter and John to minister to the new believers in Samaria?

Summary: The gospel had been welcomed by the Samaritans, but would the Samaritans be welcomed by the Jews? Or would there be separate factions of Jewish Christians and Samaritan Christians in the church of Jesus Christ? The idea may seem unthinkable in theory; in practice it might well have happened. Is it not reasonable to suggest (in view of this historical background) that, in order to avoid just such a disaster, God deliberately withheld the Spirit from these Samaritan converts? The delay was only temporary, however, until the apostles had come down to investigate, had endorsed Philip's bold policy of Samaritan evangelism, had prayed for the converts, had laid hands on them as a sign to the whole church as well as to the Samaritan converts themselves, that they were *bona fide* Christians, to be incorporated into the redeemed community on precisely the same terms as Jewish converts.

6. *Read Acts 8:26-40.* What were the factors involved in the Ethiopian eunuch's becoming a Christian?

7. What would it have been like for Philip to leave a place where so many exciting things were happening to go down a desert road?

8. What role did Scripture play in the eunuch's conversion?

9. Ethiopia was the extreme boundary of the habitable world in the hot south. How was Philip's ministry to the eunuch the beginning of the witness "to the ends of the earth"?

10. People refer to different kinds of evangelism, such as door-to-door, friendship, mass and tract evangelism. What different kinds of evangelism do you observe throughout this whole passage?

11. What principles of evangelism do you see in this passage?

Summary: The people Philip shared the good news with were different in race, rank and religion. The Samaritans were of mixed race, half-Jewish and half-Gentile, and Asiatic, while the Ethiopian was a black African, though probably a Jew by birth. As for rank, the Samaritans were presumably ordinary citizens, whereas the Ethiopian was a distinguished public servant in the employment of the Crown. Religious differences included the fact that the Samaritans revered Moses but rejected the prophets, while the Ethiopian was returning from a pilgrimage to Jerusalem and was reading one of the very prophets the Samaritans rejected. Yet despite their differences in racial origin, social class and religion, Philip presented them both with the same good news of Jesus.

Apply

■ How are you encouraged by what you are learning about the Holy Spirit?

What have you learned from this passage that might help you become a more effective witness?

How has your view of God's work in the world grown as a result of studying this passage?

Pray——————————————————————————

■ Ask God to give you a joyful confidence in the truth, power and relevance of the gospel of Jesus Christ.

7
THE CONVERSION OF SAUL

Acts 9:1-31

*I*n the two thousand years since his death and resurrection, millions have turned to Jesus. Lives have been transformed. Directions changed. But no conversion is more dramatic then that of Saul of Tarsus. His is the most famous in church history. This is the young man who approved of Stephen's brutal death and then set out to single-handedly destroy the church. He went from house to house to drag men and women off to prison because of their faith in Jesus. Then Saul met Jesus.

Yes, Saul's conversion was dramatic. He became the apostle to the Gentiles, and we today continue to reap the benefits of his life. However, though it will probably not be on a Damascus Road, we too must experience a personal encounter with Jesus Christ in order to be converted. We too must turn to him in faith and repentance and receive a call to serve Christ and his church.

Open

■ It is good to reflect on the work of God in our lives. What was it like when you became a follower of Jesus?

Study

1. *Read Acts 9:1-19.* Describe Saul according to verses 1 and 2.

Luke has already mentioned Saul three times in Acts, each time as a bitter opponent of Christ and his church. He had not changed. He was still in the same mental condition of hatred and hostility. Some of the language that Luke uses to describe Saul in his preconversion state seems deliberately to portray him as "a wild and ferocious beast."

2. Describe Saul's experience on the Damascus road.

3. If you were Saul, what do you think it would be like to meet Jesus in this way?

4. In what ways does Saul's conversion demonstrate the marvelous grace of God?

If we ask what caused Saul's conversion, only one answer is possible. What stands out from the narrative is the sovereign grace of God through Jesus

Christ. Saul did not "decide for Christ," as we might say. On the contrary, he was persecuting Christ. It was rather Christ who decided for him and intervened in his life.

To ascribe Saul's conversion to God's initiative can easily be misunderstood, however; the sovereign grace which captured Saul was neither sudden (in the sense that there had been no previous preparation) nor compulsive (in the sense that he needed to make no response). This was not the first time Jesus Christ had spoken to him. According to Paul's own words, Jesus said to him, "It is hard for you to kick against the goads" (Acts 26:14), a Greek proverb describing the useless resistance of an oxen who is being broken in.

Sovereign grace is gradual grace and gentle grace. Gradually and without violence, Jesus pricked Saul's mind and conscience. Then he revealed himself to him in a way as to enable him to make a free response. Divine grace does not trample human personality, but rather it enables human beings to be truly human. It is sin that imprisons. It is grace that liberates.

---

5. What immediate evidence of transformation do you see in Saul after his encounter with Jesus?

---

6. William Barclay calls Ananias "one of the forgotten heroes of the Christian church" (*The Acts of the Apostles* in *The Daily Study Bible* [St. Andrew Press, 1953], p. 74). What is the significance of Ananias's ministry to Saul?

7. *Read Acts 9:19-31.* Just as in Damascus, the believers in Jerusalem were afraid of Saul. What does Barnabas teach us about relating to new Christians?

8. By Paul's own testimony later in the book of Acts (26:16), on the Damascus road Jesus appointed him "as a servant and as a witness" and as the apostle to the Gentiles. How does Paul live out his responsibility to the world in this passage of Scripture?

9. What connection do you see between Saul's conversion and the church throughout Judea, Galilee and Samaria enjoying a time of peace?

Summary: Thus the story of Saul's conversion in Acts 9 begins with him leaving Jerusalem with an official mandate from the high priest to arrest fugitive Christians, and ends with him leaving Jerusalem as a persecuted Christian himself. Witness to Christ involves suffering for Christ. It is not an accident that the Greek word for witness (*martys*) came to be associated with martyrdom.

Apply —————————————————————————

■ How did your conversion compare or contrast with Saul's?

How are you continuing to experience the grace of God in your life?

How do you need to be more like Ananias and Barnabas in your church or Christian community?

How do you expect to see God working in the lives of those around you who are not Christians?

Pray

■ In silence, reflect on the miracle of your relationship with God through Jesus Christ. Thank him.

8
THE CONVERSION
OF CORNELIUS

Acts 9:32—11:18

*R*acism. Tribalism. Sexism. Cultural snobbery. Various types of discrimination have a great hold on the church and great power to destroy the unity of the body of Christ. This was as true of the early church as it is today.

Through the conversion of Cornelius, God demonstrated irrevocably that he does not make distinctions in his kingdom. Therefore we have no right to make distinctions either. The fact that we do not practice complete equality as members of the church of Christ is a blasphemy against God. Unfortunately, the early church did not hear clearly and live forever by God's message that he does not show favoritism.

Open ————————————————————————————
■ When have you felt separated from people because of cultural or racial differences?

Study

1. *Read Acts 9:32-43.* How was the power of God demonstrated in this passage?

2. What were the results of the demonstration of this power?

The miracles portrayed Peter as an authentic apostle of Jesus Christ, who performed "the signs of a true apostle." Similar miracles had endorsed the prophetic ministry of Elijah and Elisha. Four factors support this suggestion. First, both miracles followed the example of Jesus. Second, both miracles were performed by the power of Jesus. Third, both miracles were signs of the salvation of Jesus. Fourth, both miracles caused everyone to turn to the Lord.

3. *Read Acts 10:1-9.* What evidence was there in the character of Cornelius that the Holy Spirit was working in him (v. 2)?

4. What do you learn about the character of God from his response to Cornelius through the angel (vv. 3-6)?

Read Acts 10:9-23. It is difficult for us to grasp the impassable gulf which yawned in those days between the Jews on the one hand and the Gentiles (including even the "God-fearers") on the other. Not that the Old Testament itself supported such a divide. Psalmists and prophets foretold the day when God's Messiah would inherit the nations, the Lord's servant would be their light, all nations would "flow" to the Lord's house, and God would pour out his Spirit on all humankind. The tragedy was that Israel twisted the doctrine of election into one of favoritism, became filled with racial pride and hatred, and developed traditions which kept them apart. No orthodox Jew would ever enter the home of a Gentile, even a God-fearer, or invite such into his home (see v. 28).

5. How did God prepare Peter for Cornelius?

6. What would the command in verse 15 have meant to Peter?

It is interesting that Luke ended the story of Aeneas and Tabitha with the information that "Peter stayed in Joppa for some time with a tanner named Simon" (9:43). For, since tanners worked with dead animals, in order to convert their skins into leather, they were regarded as ceremonially unclean. This may have been the first sign of Peter's openness to Gentiles.

7. *Read Acts 10:24-48*. What evidence is there that Cornelius expected God to work (vv. 24-26)?

8. What would have been the consequence if Peter or Cornelius had not obeyed God?

9. What is the message that God has for Cornelius (vv. 33-43)?

Summary: Luke has now recounted the conversions of Saul and Cornelius. The differences between these two men were considerable. In race Saul was a Jew, Cornelius a Gentile; in culture Saul was a scholar, Cornelius a soldier; in religion Saul was a bigot, Cornelius a seeker. Yet both were converted by the gracious initiative of God; both received forgiveness of sins and the gift of the Spirit; and both were baptized and welcomed into the Christian family on equal terms. This fact is a signal testimony to the power and impartiality of the gospel of Christ, which is still "the power of God for the salvation of everyone who believes; first for the Jew, then for the Gentile" (Romans 1:16).

10. *Read Acts 11:1-18.* Throughout this passage we see Peter learning about God's desire for him to take the gospel to the Gentiles. Trace the process of Peter's understanding.

11. Look at this passage carefully. In what ways do you see unity growing within the church?

Apply
■ How are you affected as you see the timing and plan of God in people's lives?

How have you experienced this in your own life?

How do you see unity between people from different cultures and races lived out in your church?

Pray
■ Ask God to reveal to you bigotry in your own life and ways that you separate yourself from others because of cultural or racial differences. Ask him to change you and forgive you.

9
Growing Pains

Acts 11:19—12:24

God works in strange ways. At a time when it would seem good for the church to be together, to grow and mature, to enjoy fellowship, they are scattered all over by persecution. What were the results? The spread of the gospel. The greater the opposition the greater the expansion of the church.

There is a tendency in many of our churches today for us to want to "stay together." Mature. Become more of who we are and ignore the rest of the world. We also see that the principle that "the greater the persecution the greater the expansion" seems to apply today also.

Open ————————————————————

■ When have you seen painful circumstances in your life produce good results?

Study ————————————————————

■ *Read Acts 11:19-30.* Luke ended his previous section with the words "God has granted even the Gentiles repentance unto life" (v. 18). It was an epoch-making declaration by the conservative Jewish leaders of the Jerusalem church. The inclusion of the Gentiles is to be Luke's main theme in the rest of Acts.

---

1. What good resulted from believers' being scattered by the persecution that was connected with Stephen?

Luke now shows how the outward movement of the gospel expanded in two ways, geographical and cultural. Geographically, the mission spread north beyond "Judea and Samaria." Culturally, the mission spread beyond Jews to Gentiles. Some speculate that Luke himself was one of these converts.

---

2. What different efforts were made to nurture the new believers at Antioch?

---

3. What does it take to remain "true to the Lord" with all your heart (11:23)?

---

4. What do these efforts say about the importance of discipling young Christians?

5. Why do you think Luke makes a point of mentioning the predicted famine (11:27-30)?

Summary: It is not an accident that the Jerusalem recipients of Antiochene relief are called "brothers" (11:29). More important still, this brotherhood or family included both Jewish and Gentile believers, and the fellowship between them was illustrated in the relations between their two churches. The church of Jerusalem had sent Barnabas to Antioch; now the church of Antioch sent Barnabas, with Saul, back to Jerusalem. This famine relief anticipated the collection which Paul was later to organize, in which the affluent Greek churches of Macedonia and Achaia contributed to the needs of the impoverished churches of Judea. Its importance to Paul was that it was a symbol of Gentile-Jewish solidarity in Christ.

6. *Read Acts 12:1-24.* What do we learn about Herod in the first four verses?

7. Try to put yourself in Peter's sandals. What do you think it was like to be led out of jail by an angel?

8. How did the Christians who had gathered to pray for Peter (and who knew about James's death) respond when he appeared at the door (12:12-17)?

9. What was the cause of Herod's death (12:21-23)?

10. What are the similarities between the cause of his death and those of the death of Ananias and Sapphira (5:1-10)?

11. What does Herod's death tell you about God?

Summary: Indeed, one cannot fail to admire the artistry with which Luke depicts the complete reversal of the church's situation. At the beginning of the chapter Herod is on the rampage—arresting and persecuting church leaders; at the end he is himself struck down and dies. The chapter opens with James dead, Peter in prison and Herod triumphing; it closes with Herod dead, Peter free and the Word of God triumphing. Such is the power of God to overthrow hostile human plans and to establish his own in their place. Tyrants may be permitted for a time to boast and bluster, oppressing the church and hindering the spread of the gospel, but they will not last. In the end, their empire will be broken and their pride abased.

Apply ————————————————————————
■ What efforts are you—or could you be—making to nurture young believers?

What have you learned from this passage about how God uses suffering?

Who or what encourages you to remain true to the Lord with all your heart?

Pray

■ Ask the Holy Spirit to use the church of Jesus Christ to grow. Reflect on what it might cost you for that prayer to be answered.

10
SPREADING
THE WORD

Acts 12:25—14:28

*T*he first missionary journey was at once inspiring and terrifying. A blessing and a trial. When Paul and Barnabas returned from their journey they reported back full of excitement to the church which sent them out. God had done tremendous things: many became Christians, churches were established, elders appointed, their message affirmed by miracles and the word of God spread. They also reported of opposition from the religious leaders and being kicked out of cities and stoned, at times close to the point of death. Through it all, however, they knew they would not be stopped because the Holy Spirit sent them and went with them.

Open ────────────────────────────────

■ What do you think would be most difficult about being a missionary?

Study ────────────────────────────────

■ *Read Acts 12:25—13:4.* The previous study ended with the thrilling words "but the word of God continued to increase and spread." Now Luke has reached a decisive turning point in his narrative. In keeping with the risen Lord's prophecy (1:8), witness has been borne to him "in Jerusalem" and in "all Judea and Samaria." Now the horizon broadens to "the ends of the earth." Up to this point all the action in evangelism has been limited to the Palestinian and Syrian mainland. Nobody has yet caught the vision of taking the good news to the nations overseas (although Cyprus has been mentioned in 11:19). Now at last, however, that momentous step is to be taken.

---

1. Describe the scene in these verses.

It is unlikely that the Holy Spirit revealed his will only to the small group of five leaders, for that would entail three of them being instructed about the other two. It is more likely that the church members as a whole are in mind, since both they and the leaders are mentioned together in verse 1. Moreover, when Paul and Barnabas returned, "they gathered the church together." They reported to the church because they had been commissioned by the church.

---

2. How does the way Paul and Barnabas are sent compare and contrast with how we send off our missionaries today?

---

3. How does the church of the twenty-first century need to change in order to follow the example of the early church in missions?

Summary: Would it not be true to say that the Spirit sent them out, by instructing the church to do so, and that the church sent them out, having been directed by the Spirit to do so? This balance will be a healthy corrective to opposite extremes. The first is the tendency to individualism, by which a Christian claims direct personal guidance by the Spirit without any reference to the church. The second is the tendency to institutionalism, by which all decision-making is done by the church without any reference to the Spirit. Although we have no liberty to deny the validity of personal choice, it is safe and healthy only in relation to the Spirit and the church. Still today it is the responsibility of every local church (especially of its leaders) to be sensitive to the Holy Spirit, in order to discover who he may be gifting and calling.

---

4. *Read Acts 13:4-12.* Contrast the proconsul with Elymas the sorcerer.

---

5. Luke tells us that Paul was freshly filled with the Holy Spirit, to show that his boldness, outspokenness and power in condemning Elymas were all from God. Why do you think Paul was so severe in his reprimand of Elymas (vv. 9-11)?

Luke chooses this moment to inform us that Saul was also called Paul. It was common for Jews to take a Greek or Roman second name, and it was appropriate for Luke to mention Saul's now as he moves into increasingly non-Jewish contexts. He does not call Paul "Saul" again.

6. *Read Acts 13:13-52.* How do you see God's grace emphasized in Paul's history of Israel (vv. 16-25)?

7. Paul jumps from David to the promised Savior, Jesus. What truth about Jesus does he proclaim?

8. What are the consequences of his sermon (vv. 42-52)?

9. What do you learn from Paul and Barnabas about interacting with those who are hostile to the gospel?

Summary: Luther wrote in his *Preface to the Acts of the Apostles,* "It should be noted that by this book St. Luke teaches the whole of Christendom . . . that the true and chief article of Christian doctrine is this: We must all be justified alone by faith in Jesus Christ, without any contribution from the law or help from our works. This doctrine is the chief of the book and the author's principal reason for writing" ([Muhlenberg Press, 1960], p. 363). On the other hand, over against the offer of forgiveness, Paul issues a solemn warning to those who reject it.

10. *Read Acts 14:1-28.* How do Paul and Barnabas react to being perceived as gods (vv. 14-18)?

11. This first missionary journey illustrates the extraordinary versatility of the apostle in adapting himself to different situations; he appeared to be equally at ease with individuals and crowds, Jews and Gentiles, the religious and the irreligious, the educated and the uneducated, the friendly and the hostile. Contrast the way the people responded to Paul's message.

12. In summary, what different approaches do you see Paul take as he relates to different groups and individuals throughout this whole passage?

13. Retrace Paul and Barnabas's steps through this first missionary journey, and look for the ways they made sure that the churches they left behind had a solid foundation on which to grow (13:43, 49; 14:21-23).

Summary: The most notable feature of this first missionary journey was the missionaries' sense of divine direction. It was the Holy Spirit of God himself who told the church of Antioch to set Barnabas and Saul apart, who sent them out, who led them from place to place, and who gave power to their preaching, so that converts were made and churches planted. The sending church had committed them to the grace of God for their work (14:26), and on their return they reported "all that God had done through them and how he had opened the door of faith to the Gentiles" (14:27). True, he had done the work "with them" (literally), in cooperation or partnership with them, but he had done it, and they gave him the credit. The grace had come from him; the glory must go to him.

Apply ————————————————————————————

■ As you observe that the Holy Spirit permeates everything that Paul and Barnabas are and do, how would you like to see this more true of your life?

How would you like to see your church grow in touching the world with the gospel?

Pray ————————————————————————————

■ We are called to be missionaries, whether at home or abroad. Ask the Holy Spirit to reveal to you all that hinders you from fully responding to that call and to keep you faithful to it.

11
RESOLVING CONFLICT

Acts 15:1—16:5

Conflict between believers is one of the most difficult things we face. There are those whose total outlook on Christianity has been drastically affected as the result of a church split or Christian friends not speaking to each other.

Thankfully the Bible is not silent on conflict. It has much to offer on how to deal with conflict and differences in ideas in a godly way. Acts 15 is one such passage. The vital question of how Gentile believers would be incorporated into the believing community began to form in the mind of the Jewish Christians. This question, left unattended, could have torn the church apart. There is much of this same kind of discussion today, and the council of Jerusalem provides an excellent model for resolving our differences.

Open

■ How have you seen Christians and/or congregations deal with conflict?

Study
■ *Read Acts 15:1-21.* So far it had been assumed that Gentile believers would be absorbed into the believing community by circumcision, and that by observing the law they would be acknowledged as bona fide members of the covenant of God. Something quite different was now happening, however: Gentile converts were being welcomed into fellowship by baptism without circumcision. They were becoming Christians without becoming Jews.

1. What was the question that was forming in the minds of the Jewish leaders (vv. 1-5)?

2. Why was this issue so important?

3. What might be some comparable issues in today's church?

4. Describe carefully the process of resolving this conflict (vv. 6-21).

5. What can we learn about the resolution of a disagreement from the way the Jewish leaders worked toward resolution?

It was one thing to secure the gospel from corruption; it was another to preserve the church from fragmentation. Paul was resolutely unwilling to compromise the "truth of the gospel." At the same time, he was extremely anxious to maintain Jewish-Gentile solidarity in the one body of Christ. Once the theological principle that salvation is by grace alone and that circumcision was not required but neutral was firmly established, he was prepared to adjust his practical policies.

We may say, then, that the Jerusalem Council secured a double victory—a victory of love in preserving the fellowship by sensitive concessions to conscientious Jewish scruples. As Luther put it, Paul was strong in faith and soft in love. Or as John Newton once said, "Paul was a reed in non-essentials,—an iron pillar in essentials."

---

6. *Read Acts 15:22-35.* What do the leaders do to make sure the decisions from the council are adequately communicated to the churches?

---

7. Why do you think the Gentile believers were given a list of four behaviors from which to abstain, even though they did not have to be circumcised or obey the law of Moses to be saved (vv. 28-29)?

---

8. *Read Acts 15:36—16:5.* How did Paul and Barnabas deal with their sharp disagreement about whether or not to take John Mark with them on their next missionary journey?

9. How do you respond to how they resolved this conflict?

10. After all the discussion in the council at Jerusalem about Gentiles not having to be circumcised, why do you think Paul circumcised Timothy before taking him along on the journey with Silas and himself?

11. How would you evaluate the spiritual health of the churches at this point?

Summary: From our later perspective of church history we can see the crucial importance of this first ecumenical Council held in Jerusalem. Its unanimous decision liberated the gospel from its Jewish swaddling clothes into being God's message for all humankind, and gave the Jewish-Gentile church a self-conscious identity as the reconciled people of God, the one body of Christ. And although the whole council affirmed it, Paul claimed that it was a new understanding granted especially to him, the "mystery" previously hidden but now revealed, namely that through faith in Christ alone Gentiles stand on equal terms with Jews as "heirs together, members together, sharers together" in his one new community.

Apply

■ Consider the principles of conflict resolution revealed in this passage. Which of them is easiest for you?

Which is most difficult?

In what ways do you need to care more for the growth and well-being of other believers?

Pray———————————————————————————
■ Praise God that we as Christians have the message of reconciliation. Ask him to soften your heart and help you to live out this message in the world.

12
FOLLOWING
THE SPIRIT

Acts 16:6—17:15

God had appointments for Paul with individuals in Macedonia. The first was with Lydia at the river on a Saturday afternoon. The second was with a slave girl who earned money for her owner by telling the future, and the third was with a jailor and his family at Philippi. Getting him to those appointments was not easy, but the Holy Spirit got them there. To do this, he closed some doors of opportunity and opened others. Paul overcame human barriers when he took the gospel to these individuals. There now was no difference between Jew and Greek, male and female, slave or free—when it came to the gospel of Christ.

We do not have to beg the Holy Spirit to guide us. But like Paul, we need to seek that guidance as we are faithful to what we already know to be God's will and as we trust God even when we cannot explain what he is doing.

Open ———————————————————————

■ What are your greatest fears about being guided by God?

The most notable feature of Paul's second missionary expedition, which Luke narrates in these chapters, is that during it the good seed of the gospel was now for the first time planted in European soil. It was from Europe that in due course the gospel fanned out to the great continents of Africa, Asia, North America, Latin America and Oceania and so reached the ends of the earth.

1. *Read Acts 16:6-15.* What specific instructions and direction did Paul and his companions receive from the Holy Spirit?

2. How do you see the Holy Spirit honor and work through their obedience throughout this passage?

3. What principles of guidance do you see in the experience of Paul and his companions?

In *The Acts of the Holy Spirit* A. T. Pierson gave some examples from the history of missions of this same kind of guidance: Livingstone tried to go to China, but God sent him to Africa instead. Before him, Carey planned to go to Polynesia in the South Seas, but God guided him to India. Judson went to India first, but was driven on to Burma. We too in our day, Pierson concludes, "need to trust him for guidance and rejoice equally in his restraints and constraints" ([Marshall, Morgan and Scott, 1895], pp. 120-22).

---

4. When have you experienced guidance in the way that Paul and Silas did?

---

5. *Read Acts 16:16-40.* What opposition was there to Paul and his message?

---

6. What was the motivation behind the owners of the slave girl dragging Paul and Silas to the authorities (vv. 19-21)?

---

7. Describe Paul and Silas's response to being flogged and thrown into prison (vv. 25-28).

8. Why do you think the jailer asked the question "What must I do to be saved?"

9. How does the response of the jailer (vv. 31-34) compare to Lydia's response to the gospel (vv. 14-15, 40)?

What does this tell you about the nature of the gospel?

10. Think of the three individuals (Lydia, a businesswoman; the slave girl and the jail keeper) who probably became Christians and were the core of the new Philippian church. How does this new church demonstrate the unifying power of the gospel?

11. The book of Acts demonstrates God's desire to reach individuals as well as the world. What would have been the consequence if Paul had not responded to the Macedonia call?

12. *Read Acts 17:1-15.* What verbs describe Paul's approach to the Thessalonians and their response (vv. 1-4)?

What verbs describe the response of the Bereans to Paul's teaching (vv. 11-12)?

13. Compare and contrast the response of the Thessalonians and the Bereans to the gospel.

Summary: It was inevitable in Jewish evangelism that the Old Testament Scriptures should be both the textbook and the court of appeal. What is impressive is that neither speaker nor hearers used Scripture in a superficial way. On the contrary, Paul "argues" out of the Scripture and the Bereans "examined" them to see if his arguments were cogent. And we may be sure that Paul welcomed and encouraged this thoughtful response. He believed in doctrine (his message had theological content), but not in indoctrination (tyrannical instruction demanding uncritical acceptance). Thus Paul's arguments and his hearers' studies went hand in hand. I do not doubt that he also bathed both in prayer, asking the Holy Spirit of truth to open his mouth to explain, and his hearers' minds to grasp, the good news of salvation in Christ.

Apply

■ How have you witnessed the power of the gospel to change lives?

How might God be guiding you to serve him?

Pray————————————————————————

■ Quietly reflect on how God has led you in the past. Thank him for his faithfulness. Commit your present and future to him now. Talk to him about your fears, desires and commitment to following him.

13
CITY OF IDOLS

Acts 17:16-34

*I*dols are not limited to primitive societies; there are many sophisticated idols too. An idol is a God substitute. Any person or thing that occupies the place which God should occupy is an idol. Covetousness is idolatry. Ideologies can be idolatries. So can fame, wealth and power, sex, food, alcohol and other drugs. People can be idols—parents, spouse, children and friends. The possibilities extend further to work, recreation, television and possessions. Even church, religion and Christian service can be idolized.

Idols seem particularly dominant in cities. Paul was deeply pained by the idolatrous city of Athens. It was a city of aesthetic magnificence and cultural sophistication, as well as being the world center of pagan philosophy and religion. How do we communicate Jesus Christ to such a city? Paul gave us a marvelous example when he visited Athens.

Open

■ What philosophies and pagan religions do you encounter in your world?

Study

1. *Read Acts 17:16-34.* What caught Paul's attention immediately about Athens?

What did he feel about what he saw?

The clue to interpreting the nature of Paul's emotion is that the verb that is translated "greatly distressed" is also used in the Greek version of the Old Testament to describe the reaction of the Holy One of Israel to idolatry. Thus, when the Israelites made the golden calf at Mount Sinai, and when later they were guilty of gross idolatry and immorality in relation to the Baal of Peor, they "provoked" the Lord God to anger. So Paul was "provoked" (RSV) by idolatry and provoked to anger, grief and indignation, just as God is himself, and for the same reason, namely for the honor and glory of his name.

2. Jesus wept over the impenitent city of Jerusalem. What are the idols in your city?

3. What did Paul do in response to what he saw and felt?

4. It is impressive that Paul was able to speak with equal ease to religious people in the synagogue, to casual passers-by in the city square and to highly sophisticated philosophers. How does Paul open his sermon at the meeting of the Areopagus (vv. 22-23)?

5. What does his approach to the men and women of the Aeropagus model to us as we consider influencing those in our culture with the message about Jesus?

6. What five things does Paul say about God?

7. What is the significance to the people of Athens that God is the Creator of the universe (vv. 24-27)?

8. Why was it important for Paul to tell the people that God is the Sustainer of life (v. 28)?

9. How did Paul call them to repentance (vv. 29-31)?

10. What different responses to Paul's message do you see throughout this passage?

11. Compare and contrast the responses to Paul's message about Jesus to the responses you see today.

Summary: The Areopagus address reveals the comprehensiveness of Paul's message. He proclaimed God in his fullness as Creator, Sustainer, Ruler, Father and Judge. He took in the whole of nature and of history. He passed the whole of time in review, from the creation to the consummation. He emphasized the greatness of God, not only as the beginning and the end of all things, but as the One to whom we owe our being and to whom we must give account. He argued that human beings already know these things by natural or general revelation, and that their ignorance and idolatry are therefore inexcusable. So he called on them with great solemnity, before it was too late, to repent.

Apply ——————————————————————————
■ When have you been provoked by the idolatrous cities of the contemporary world?

It is not only the comprehensiveness of Paul's message in Athens which is impressive, however, but also the depth and power of his motivation. Why is it that, in spite of the great needs and opportunities of our day, the church slumbers peacefully on, and that so many Christians are deaf and dumb, deaf to Christ's commission and tongue-tied in testimony? I think the major reason is this: we do not speak as Paul spoke because we do not feel as Paul felt. And this is because we do not see like Paul. When Paul walked around Athens, he did not just "notice" the idols. He looked and looked, and thought and thought, until the fires of holy indignation were kindled within him. For he saw men and women, created by God in the image of God, giving to idols the homage which was due to God alone. We constantly pray "Hallowed be your Name," but we do not seem to mean it, or to care that his name is so widely profaned.

What might it take for the church of Jesus Christ to wake up today?

Pray ————————————————————————————————
■ Ask God to give you eyes to see where he is being replaced by things and philosophies and to respond to what you see with a passion to proclaim truth and to honor his name.

14
GOOD NEWS STRATEGY

Acts 18—19

*A*s we watch Paul travel and proclaim the good news of Christ, we see a pattern that he follows when he enters each city. It is no different in Corinth and Ephesus. His first attempt is to persuade the Jews concerning Jesus. He begins in the synagogue where they meet, study Scripture and pray. But when the Jews reject his message he turns to the Gentiles. In both cities Paul's bold step of going to the Gentiles was vindicated by many people hearing and believing the gospel.

A well-thought-through strategy is vital if we are to engage the world with the message that can change it.

Open —————————————————————————————

■ How does the idea of having a strategy for evangelism strike you?

Study —————————————————————————————

1. *Read Acts 18:1-18.* What do you learn about Paul in 18:1-4?

2. What drastic action did Paul take when the Jews resisted his message this time (18:6-7)?

What are the consequences (vv. 8-10, 12-15)?

---

3. If you were Paul, how would you have felt when you received Jesus' message in verses 9-10?

How did Paul respond?

Summary: This message is couched in the language used by God himself in the Old Testament when addressing his servants. Both the prohibition "Do not be afraid" and the promise "I am with you" were repeatedly given. Now Jesus said the same things to Paul. He was to continue witnessing fortified by the presence and the protection of Christ, and by the assurance that Christ had in Corinth "many people." They had not yet believed in him, but they would do so, because already according to his purpose they belonged to him.

This conviction is the greatest of all encouragements to an evangelist. Strengthened by it, Paul stayed for a year and a half in Corinth, teaching them the word of God (18:11). For the word of God is the divinely appointed means by which people come to put their trust in Christ and so identify themselves as his.

Read Acts 18:18-28. Paul left Corinth accompanied by Priscilla and Aquila and went to Ephesus, left Priscilla and Aquila there and continued to travel throughout the area where he had gone on one of his first missionary journeys. His purpose was to strengthen the disciples.

---

4. What do you learn about Apollos in 18:24-28?

---

5. How is Aquila and Priscilla's response to him an example to us?

---

6. *Read Acts 19:1-22.* As you look through these verses, what good fruit do you see from Paul's ministry in Ephesus?

---

7. What opposition did Paul encounter?

---

8. *Read Acts 19:23-41.* What were the stated reasons and the real reason for the opposition (19:23-34)?

9. What is the significance of the fact that this is the second time (first in Corinth and now in Ephesus) that the Roman law protected Paul in his ministry?

Summary: Luke wanted to show that Rome had no case against Christianity in general or Paul in particular. In Corinth the proconsul Gallio had refused even to hear the Jews' charge. In Ephesus the town clerk implied that the opposition was purely emotional and that the Christians, being innocent, had nothing to fear from duly constituted legal processes. Thus the impartiality of Gallio, the friendship of Asiarchs and the cool reasonableness of the city clerk combined to give the gospel freedom to continue on its victorious course.

10. In spite of the obvious cultural differences between first-century cities in the Roman Empire and the great urban complexes of today, there are also similarities. What lessons can we learn from Paul's ministry in Corinth and Ephesus about the how, the where and the when of urban evangelism?

Summary: When we contrast much contemporary evangelism with Paul's, its shallowness is immediately shown up. Our evangelism tends to be focused on simply inviting people to church. Paul also took the gospel out into the secular world. Our evangelism appeals to the emotions for a decision without an adequate basis of understanding. Paul taught, reasoned and tried to persuade. Our evangelism is superficial, making brief encounters and expecting quick results. Paul stayed in Corinth and Ephesus for five years, faithfully sowing gospel seed and in due time reaping a harvest.

Apply

■ The term *tentmaker* comes from the fact that Paul worked as a tentmaker on his second missionary journey. What are reasons for tentmakers in modern missions?

How does this story of Paul at Corinth and Ephesus challenge you to become a more effective proclaimer of the gospel?

Pray

■ Thank the Lord Jesus that he will help you grow as a messenger of his truth.

15
SAYING GOODBYE

Acts 20:1—21:17

When Paul said goodbye to the leaders at Ephesus, it was the only address in Acts to a Christian audience. The leaders that are addressed are called "elders," "pastors" and "overseers." In our day when there is much confusion about the nature and purpose of the pastoral ministry, and much questioning about whether clergy are primarily social workers, psychotherapists, educators, facilitators or administrators, it is important to rehabiliate the noble word *pastors*. They are the shepherds of Christ's sheep, called to tend, feed and protect.

Paul had taken his call as pastor seriously. He had poured his life into the Ephesians, lived well before them and was now leaving them, putting the care of the church in their hands.

Open

■ Describe a time when you said a painful goodbye.

Study

1. *Read Acts 20:1-12.* In 20:1-5 what characteristics of Paul's ministry do you see?

I imagine that Paul's encouragement took the form of an exhortation similar to the one he would later give to their pastors in Miletus. It is noteworthy that Paul hardly ever traveled alone, and that when he was alone, he expressed his longing for human companionship. That he favored team-work is specially clear during his missionary journeys. On this journey he was accompanied by men that represented each of the areas he had ministered to and would be visiting.

2. How do you think you would have been affected by the worship service at Troas (20:7-12)?

3. *Read Acts 20:13-38.* How would you describe the tone of this passage?

4. How did Paul describe himself and his ministry among the Ephesians (20:18-35)?

5. How was Paul affected by the warnings of future suffering and death (20:22-24)?

6. What does he instruct the Christian leaders to do (20:28-31)?

---

7. What does Paul's instructions about the sheep he is leaving in their care communicate about their value (20:28)?

---

8. Why was Paul not afraid to leave the leaders and the church in their care?

Summary: Each of the three persons of the Trinity has a share in overseeing the church. To begin with, the church is "God's church." Next, we read that he bought it with his own blood—the blood of Christ. And over this church the Holy Spirit appoints overseers. This splendid Trinitarian affirmation should humble us to remember that the church is not ours, but God's. And it should inspire us to faithfulness. The people of the church are the flock of God the Father, purchased by the precious blood of God the Son, and supervised by overseers appointed by God the Holy Spirit. If the three persons of the Trinity are thus committed to the welfare of the people, should we not be also?

From Richard Baxter's great book *The Reformed Pastor:*
Oh then, let us hear these arguments of Christ, wherever we feel ourselves grow dull and careless: "Did I die for them, and wilt not thou look after them? Were they worth my blood and are they not worth thy labor? Did I come down from heaven to earth, to seek and to save that which was lost; and wilt thou not go to the next door or

street or village to seek them? How small is thy labor and conde-
scension as to mine? I debased myself to this, but it is thy honor to
be so employed. Have I done and suffered so much for their salvation;
and was I willing to make thee a co-worker with me, and wilt thou
refuse that little that lieth upon thy hands?

---

9. *Read Acts 21:1-17.* What continued warnings did Paul receive about
going to Jerusalem?

---

10. How did he respond to those warnings?

---

11. How do you think those observing Paul were affected by his single-
mindedness?

Summary: What fortified Paul in his journey was the Christian fellowship
which he and his travel companions experienced in every port. He was
personally escorted from Caesarea by disciples to Jerusalem where he was
received warmly. It would be an exaggeration to call this Paul's "triumphal
entry" into Jerusalem. But at least his warm reception strengthened him to
bear the crowd's shouts a few days later "Away with him!"

Apply ————————————————————————
■ How do your priorities compare and contrast with those of Paul?

What would you like to be able to say about yourself and about your ministry at the end of your life?

What steps do you need to take now in order for that to happen?

Pray ─────────────────────────────────────

■ Praise the Holy Spirit for his faithfulness in pointing us to Jesus. Ask him to stir your heart toward single-mindedness in obedience to Jesus and living a life whose total purpose is to bring glory to his name.

16
POLITICS & RELIGION

Acts 21:18—23:35

*T*he future of the gospel was at stake, as powerful forces raged for and against it. On the one hand, the Jewish persecutors were prejudiced and violent. On the other hand, the Romans were open-minded and went out of their way to maintain the standards of law, justice and order of which their best leaders were understandably proud.

Between these two powers, religious and civil, hostile and friendly, Jerusalem and Rome, Paul found himself trapped, unarmed and totally vulnerable. One cannot help admiring his courage, especially when he stood on the steps of Fortress Antonia, facing an angry crowd which had just severely manhandled him, with no power but the Word and the Spirit of God. The source of his courage was his serene confidence in the truth. And he knew that his Lord and Savior was with him and would keep his promise that he would bear witness someday, somehow, in Rome.

Open ————————————————————————

■ What examples of religious and political conflict throughout the world do you know of?

Study

1. *Read Acts 21:18-26.* Paul and his companions have been received warmly at Jerusalem. In your own words, describe the interaction between Paul and James.

2. To what extent were both men willing to go for the sake of Jewish-Gentile solidarity?

3. Though they were willing to make concessions when it came to cultural and traditional practice, was there any difference between them doctrinally and ethically? Explain.

4. How willing are you, would you say, to compromise on the nonessentials of the faith for the purpose of solidarity with your Christian brothers and sisters?

Summary: We have already seen Paul's conciliatory spirit in accepting the Jerusalem decrees and circumcising Timothy. Now, in the same tolerant spirit, he was prepared to undergo some purification rituals in order to pacify Jewish scruples. James seems to have gone too far in expecting Paul to live "in obedience to the law" in all matters and at all times, if that was what he meant (21:24). But Paul was certainly ready to do so for the sake of Jewish-Gentile solidarity. According to Paul's conviction, Jewish cultural practices belonged to the "matters indifferent," from which he had been liberated, but which he might or might not himself practice according to the circumstances.

James manifested a similarly sweet and generous mind both by praising God for the Gentile mission and by accepting the offering from the Gentile churches. The unbending prejudice and fanatical violence of the unbelieving Jews, which Luke now describes, stands out in ugly contrast to the cooperation between Paul and James.

---

5. *Read Acts 21:27-36.* What two accusations are made against Paul by the angry crowd?

---

6. How were these accusations both inaccurate and ironical?

The Jews misunderstood both Stephen and Paul, just as they had misunderstood Jesus. Jesus spoke of himself as the fulfillment of the temple, the people and the law, and Stephen and Paul followed suit. This was not to denigrate them, however, but to reveal their true glory.

Gentiles were permitted to enter only the outer court, the Court of the Gentiles. According to Josephus, beyond this, and preventing access into the Court of Israel, there was "a stone wall for a partition," four and a half feet high, "with an inscription which forbade any foreigner to go in under pain of death." The Roman government had given the Jews permission to kill any non-Jews who went beyond the barricade, even Roman citizens. Paul was surely thinking of this barrier when he wrote of "the dividing wall of hostility" between Jews and Gentiles.

7. *Read Acts 21:37—22:29.* In what ways did Paul demonstrate sensitivity to the crowd as he boldly made his speech of defense?

In 22:22 Paul is interrupted by the crowd, who demanded his death. In the eyes of Jews proselytism (making Gentiles into Jews) was fine; but evangelism (making Gentiles into Christians without first making them Jews) was an abomination. It was tantamount to saying that Jews and Gentiles were equal, for they both needed to come to God through Christ, and that on identical terms.

8. How do Roman law and justice come to Paul's aid (22:24-29)?

9. *Read Acts 22:30—23:35.* Ananias ordered Paul to be struck in the mouth when he said, "My brothers, I have fulfilled my duty to God in all good conscience to this day" (23:1-2). What was Paul claiming about himself?

10. How does your own purpose in life compare with Paul's statement?

11. What is the source of the conflict between the Sadducees and the Pharisees (23:6-10)?

12. What effect do you think the Lord's appearance and message had on Paul as you consider what he had been through and what he had yet to face?

13. How do you see God continuing to protect Paul in 23:12-35?

Apply

■ In what ways are you like and unlike Paul in your response when you are falsely accused?

In what ways would you like to emulate Paul in your commitment to the gospel of Christ?

What do you need for this to happen?

Pray

■ Ask God to help you to listen long and hard before you speak to those you disagree with, both Christians and others.

17
THE GOSPEL ON TRIAL

Acts 24—26

*J*erusalem and Rome were the centers of two enormously strong power blocs. The faith of Jerusalem went back two millennia to Abraham. The rule of Rome extended some three million square miles around the Mediterranean Sea. Jerusalem's strength lay in history and tradition, Rome's in conquest and organization. Their combined might was overwhelming. If a solitary dissident like Paul were to set himself against them, the outcome could be inevitable. His chances of survival would resemble those of a butterfly before a steamroller. He would be crushed, utterly obliterated from the face of the earth.

Yet such an outcome, we may confidently affirm, never even entered Paul's mind as a possibility. For he saw the situation from an entirely different perspective. He was no traitor to either church or state, that he should come into collision with them, although this is how his accusers tried to frame him. Paul's contention, while on trial, was that in principle the gospel both supports the rule of Caesar and fulfills the hope of Israel. He presents himself as both a loyal citizen of Rome and a loyal son of Israel.

The gospel is on trial today. May we share the confidence and courage of Paul as we live and speak its defense.

Open

■ How do you feel/respond when you know of or experience injustice in a court system?

Study

■ In the previous chapter Felix had read the letter from Claudius Lysias and sent to Jerusalem for Paul's accusers. In the meantime he kept him in custody in Caesarea. Five days later the high priest came and opened the prosecution.

Read Acts 24. As a trained and experienced professional lawyer, Tertullus began with an endeavor to capture the judge's good will. Traditionally, it was complimentary to the point of hypocrisy and often included a promise of brevity, but on this occasion it descended to "almost nauseating flattery." For Tertullus expressed gratitude for the "peace" Felix had secured and the "reforms" he had introduced, whereas in reality he had put down several insurrections with such barbarous brutality that he earned for himself the horror, not the thanks, of the Jewish population.

---

1. What three charges did Tertullus make against Paul (24:5-6)?

---

2. How did Paul speak to each of the accusations?

3. What four affirmations does he state in 24:14-16?

---

4. Why did Felix not come to any decision about Paul (24:26-27)?

Summary: Drusilla, the wife of Felix, was the youngest daughter of Herod Agrippa I, whose opposition and death Luke has described earlier (12:1-23). She had a reputation for ravishing youthful beauty, on account of which Felix, with the aid of a Cypriot magician, had seduced her from her rightful husband and secured her for himself. She was in fact his third wife. The lax morals of Felix and Drusilla help to explain the topics Paul addressed.

There was to be no further public hearing for two years. During this period, however, Felix conducted a kind of private investigation of his own. He frequently sent for Paul and talked with him. Luke is explicit that he hoped for a bribe. It would be cynical to suppose, however, that Felix's only motive was to hold Paul for ransom. I think he knew that Paul had something more precious than money, something which money cannot buy. If his conscience had been aroused by Paul's teaching, then he must have been seeking forgiveness and peace. Certainly the release of Felix from sin meant more to Paul than his own release from prison. But unfortunately there is no evidence that Felix ever capitulated to Christ and was redeemed. On the contrary, Felix left Paul in prison for his successor.

---

5. *Read Acts 25:1-22.* What kind of a person do think Festus is based on the description of him and his actions in chapter 25?

6. Why do you think Paul requested to be tried in Caesar's court (25:10-11)?

---

7. In Festus's report to Agrippa, what is the main point about Christianity that he mentions (25:18-19)?

Herod Agrippa II was the son of Herod Agrippa I and the great-grandson of Herod the Great. Bernice was his sister, and rumors were rife that their relationship was incestuous. Paul's trial before Agrippa is the longest and most elaborate.

Read Acts 25:23—26:32. It was a dramatic moment when the holy and humble apostle of Jesus Christ stood before this representative of the worldly, ambitious, morally corrupt family of the Herods who for generation after generation had set themselves in opposition to truth and righteousness. "Their founder, Herod the Great," wrote R. B. Rackham in The Acts of the Apostles, "had tried to destroy the infant Jesus." His son Antipas, the tetrarch of Galilee, beheaded John the Baptist, and won from the Lord the title of "fox." His grandson Agrippa I slew James the son of Zebedee with the sword. Now we see Paul brought before Agrippa's son. But Paul was not the least intimidated.

---

8. Why does Paul say that he is on trial (26:6-8)?

9. What are the main points about himself that Paul highlights for King Agrippa?

---

10. What is Paul's commission from Jesus Christ according to 26:15-18?

The commissioning of Saul as Christ's apostle was deliberately shaped to resemble the call of Isaiah, Ezekiel, Jeremiah and others to be God's prophets. In both cases the language of "sending" was used. As God "sent" his prophets to announce his word to his people, so Christ "sent" apostles to preach and teach in his name, including Paul, who was now "sent" to the Gentiles.

---

11. How is Paul's heart's desire and commitment to this commission again communicated in his final interaction with Agrippa in 26:26-29?

Summary: Luke's purpose in describing the three court scenes was not just apologetic, but evangelistic. He wanted his readers to remember that Paul had been commissioned to be Christ's servant and witness. Thank God for Paul's courage! Jesus had warned his disciples that they would be "brought before kings and governors" on account of his name, and had promised that on such occasions he would give them "words and wisdom" (Luke 21:12-15). Jesus had also told Ananias (who had presumably passed the information on) that Paul was his "chosen instrument" to carry his name "before the Gentiles and their kings and before the people of Israel" (Acts 9:15). These predictions had

come true, and Paul had not failed. Christ had commissioned him personally and directly, and he had not been disobedient to this heavenly vision!

Apply ———————————————————————

■ What do you think that most people remember about Christianity from
your witness?

To what degree is Paul's commission from Jesus Christ your own?

Pray ———————————————————————

■ Thank God for the gift of the Holy Spirit. Ask the Holy Spirit to place in
you a burning desire that your friends come to Christ.

18
FOLLOWING GOD'S LEAD

Acts 27–28

*R*ome, the largest and most splendid of ancient cities, acted like a magnet to its peoples. Rome, the capital and symbol of the Roman Empire, presided magisterially over the whole known world. Though Paul was a Jew, but having inherited Roman citizenship from his father, he must have dreamed since childhood of visiting the city for himself. Paul must have thought often of what it would be like for this great city to be thoroughly evangelized, and for Rome's church to grow, be consolidated and fired with a missionary vision. What a radiating center for the gospel Rome could become!

Open
■ What dreams do you have concerning taking the gospel to others?

Study
1. *Read Acts 27.* What did Paul and the others have to go through to get to Rome?

2. How do you see Paul reaching out to those around him while they travel to Rome (vv. 9-10, 21-26, 31-36)?

---

3. Paul had great confidence in God, and many others were profoundly affected by it. What promises from God were the foundation for Paul's great confidence that they would all arrive safely in Rome (vv. 23-26)?

---

4. What kind of care and respect did Paul receive from Julius the centurion (vv. 3, 43)?

---

5. What does this relationship with Julius tell you about the apostle Paul?

Summary: Here then are aspects of Paul's character which endear him to us as an integrated Christian, who combined spirituality with sanity and faith with works. He believed that God would keep his promises and had the courage to say grace in the presence of a crowd of hard-bitten pagans. But his trust and godliness did not stop him seeing either that the ship should not take risks with the onset of winter or that the sailors must not be allowed to escape, or that the hungry crew and passengers had to eat to survive. What a man! He was a man of God and of action, a man of the Spirit and of common sense.

6. *Read Acts 28.* Paul dealt with many fickle crowds in his journey. How is the fickleness of this crowd displayed (28:1-6)?

7. What kindnesses are exchanged between the islanders and Paul (28:2, 10)?

8. What do you think it was like for Paul to be met by a delegation of Christians when he finally arrived in Rome (28:14-15)?

9. Paul continued to follow the principle that the gospel is for the Jew first, even in the Gentile capital of Rome. How did the Jews respond?

10. What do you think it means that "boldly and without hindrance" (28:31) Paul preached the kingdom of God and taught about the Lord Jesus Christ?

Summary: What, then, is the major lesson we are intended to learn from Acts 27 and 28? It concerns the providence of God, who "works out everything in conformity with the purpose of his will" (Ephesians 1:11). This providential activity of God is seen in these chapters in two complementary ways, first in bringing Paul to Rome, his desired goal, and second in bringing him there as a prisoner, his undesired condition.

It was not so much that Paul had said, "I must visit Rome" (19:21), as that Jesus had said to him, "You must testify in Rome" (23:11). Yet circumstance after circumstance seemed calculated to make this impossible. As the narrative proceeds and the storm becomes ever more violent, until all hope is lost, we wonder how on earth he will be rescued. Will he make it? Yes he will! He does! By God's providence Paul reached Rome safe and sound.

Apply

■ Many were profoundly affected by Paul's confidence in God. When have you been influenced by such confidence in another believer?

What have you learned from the book of Acts that prepares and equips you to be a witness "to the ends of the earth" (1:8)?

Just as Luke's Gospel ended with the prospect of a mission to the nations, so the Acts ends with the prospect of a mission radiating from Rome to the world. Luke's description of Paul preaching "with boldness" and "without hindrance" symbolizes a wide open door, through which we in our day have to pass. The Acts of the Apostles have long ago finished. But the acts of the followers of Jesus will continue until the end of the world, and their words will spread to the ends of the earth.

Pray

■ Pray fervently that God will empower you with his Holy Spirit to do his will.

Guidelines for Leaders

My grace is sufficient for you. (2 Corinthians 12:9)
   If leading a small group is something new for you, don't worry. These sessions are designed to be led easily. Because the Bible study questions flow from observation to interpretation to application, you may feel as if the studies lead themselves.

   You don't need to be an expert on the Bible or a trained teacher to lead a small group discussion. As a leader, you can guide group members to discover for themselves what the Bible has to say and to listen for God's guidance. This method of learning will allow group members to remember much more of what is said than a lecture would.

   This study guide is flexible. You can use it with a variety of groups—students, professionals, neighborhood or church groups. Each study takes forty-five to sixty minutes in a group setting.

   There are some important facts to know about group dynamics and encouraging discussion. The suggestions listed below should equip you to effectively and enjoyably fulfill your role as leader.

Preparing for the Study

   1. Ask God to help you understand and apply the passage in your own life. Unless this happens, you will not be prepared to lead others. Pray too for the various members of the group. Ask God to open your hearts to the message of his Word and motivate you to action.

   2. Read the introduction to the entire guide to get an overview of the topics that will be explored.

   3. As you begin each study, read and reread the assigned Bible passage to familiarize yourself with it.

4. This study guide is based on the New International Version of the Bible. It will help you and the group if you use this translation as the basis for your study and discussion.

5. Carefully work through each question in the study. Spend time in meditation and reflection as you consider how to respond.

6. Write your thoughts and responses in the space provided in the study guide. This will help you to express your understanding of the passage clearly.

7. You may want to get a copy of the Bible Speaks Today commentary by John Stott that supplements the Bible book you are studying. The commentary is divided into short units on each section of Scripture so you can easily read the appropriate material each week. This will help you answer tough questions about the passage and its context.

It may help to have a Bible dictionary handy. Use it to look up any unfamiliar words, names or places. (For additional help on how to study a passage, see *How to Lead a LifeGuide Bible Study* from InterVarsity Press, USA.)

8. Take the "Apply" portion of each study seriously. Consider how you need to apply the Scripture to your life. Remember that the group members will follow your lead in responding to the studies. They will not go any deeper than you do.

Leading the Study

1. Begin the study on time. Open with prayer, asking God to help the group to understand and apply the passage.

2. Be sure that everyone in your group has a study guide. Encourage the group to prepare beforehand for each discussion by reading the introduction to the guide and by working through the questions in each study.

3. At the beginning of your first time together, explain that these studies are meant to be discussions, not lectures. Encourage the members of the group to participate. However, do not put pressure on those who may be hesitant to speak during the first few sessions.

4. Have a group member read aloud the introduction at the beginning of the discussion.

5. Every session begins with an "open" question, which is meant to be asked before the passage is read. These questions are designed to introduce the theme of the study and encourage group members to begin to open up. Encourage as many members as possible to participate, and be ready to get the discussion going with your own response.

These opening questions can reveal where our thoughts or feelings need to be transformed by Scripture. That is why it is especially important not to read the passage before the question is asked. The passage will tend to color the honest reactions people would otherwise give because they are, of course, supposed to think the way the Bible does.

6. Have a group member read aloud the passage to be studied.

7. As you ask the study questions, keep in mind that they are designed to be used just as they are written. You may simply read them aloud. Or you may prefer to express them in your own words.

There may be times when it is appropriate to deviate from the study guide. For example, a question may have already been answered. If so, move on to the next question. Or someone may raise an important question not covered in the guide. Take time to discuss it, but try to keep the group from going off on tangents.

8. Avoid answering your own questions. If necessary repeat or rephrase them until they are clearly understood. Or point the group to the commentary woven into the guide to clarify the context or meaning without answering the question. An eager group quickly becomes passive and silent if members think the leader will do most of the talking.

9. Don't be afraid of silence in response to the discussion questions. People may need time to think about the question before formulating their answers.

10. Don't be content with just one answer. Ask, "What do the rest of you think?" or "Anything else?" until several people have given answers to the question.

11. Acknowledge all contributions. Try to be affirming whenever possible. Never reject an answer. If it is clearly off-base, ask, "Which verse led you to that conclusion?" or again, "What do the rest of you think?"

12. Don't expect every answer to be addressed to you, even though this will probably happen at first. As group members become more at ease, they will begin to truly interact with each other. This is one sign of healthy discussion.

13. Don't be afraid of controversy. It can be very stimulating. If you don't resolve an issue completely, don't be frustrated. Explain that the group will move on and God may enlighten all of you in later sessions.

14. Periodically summarize what the group has said about the passage. This helps to draw together the various ideas mentioned and gives continuity to the study. But don't preach.

15. Conclude your time together with conversational prayer, adapting the prayer suggestion at the end of the study to your group. Ask for God's help in following through on the commitments you've made.

16. End on time.

Many more suggestions and helps can be found in *How to Lead a LifeGuide Bible Study* and *The Big Book on Small Groups* (both from InterVarsity Press, USA) or *Housegroups* (Crossway Books, UK). Reading through one of these books would be worth your time.

For Further Reading from InterVarsity Press

The Bible Speaks Today by John Stott
The books in this practical and readable series are companions to the John Stott Bible Studies. They provide further background and insight into the passages.

The Message of Acts
The Message of Ephesians
The Message of Galatians
The Message of Romans (UK title), *Romans* (US title)
The Message of the Sermon on the Mount (Matthew 5—7)
The Message of 1 & 2 Thessalonians
The Message of 1 Timothy & Titus (UK title), *Guard the Truth* (US title)
The Message of 2 Timothy